FREEDOM
STUDY GUIDE

Copyright © 2023 by Jason Hanash

Published by Arrows & Stones

All rights reserved. No portion of this book may be reproduced, stored in a retrieval system, or transmitted in any form or by any means—electronic, mechanical, photocopy, recording, scanning, or other—except for brief quotations in critical reviews or articles, without prior written permission of the author.

Unless otherwise noted, all Scripture quotations are taken from the Holy Bible, New International Version®, NIV®. Copyright © 1973, 1978, 1984, 2011 by Biblica, Inc.™ Used by permission of Zondervan. All rights reserved worldwide. www.zondervan.com. The "NIV" and "New International Version" are trademarks registered in the United States Patent and Trademark Office by Biblica, Inc.™

For foreign and subsidiary rights, contact the author.

Cover design by: Sara Young

ISBN: 978-1-960678-58-4   1 2 3 4 5 6 7 8 9 10

Printed in the United States of America

FREEDOM
STUDY GUIDE

8 Steps to
Healing and Transformation

JASON HANASH

CONTENTS

STEP 1. Dealing with the Prison of our Past 6

STEP 2. Knowing My True Identity 10

STEP 3. Choosing Relationship Over Religion 14

STEP 4. Breaking the Cycle of Generational Curses 18

STEP 5. Hearing God's Voice 22

STEP 6. Mastering Your Mind 26

STEP 7. Opposing a Culture of Idolatry 30

STEP 8. Using Spiritual Weapons for a Spiritual War 36

STEP 1

DEALING WITH THE PRISON OF OUR PAST

When you hold on to your history, you do so at the expense of your destiny.

READING TIME

As you read Step 1: "Dealing with the Prison of Our Past" in *Freedom*, reflect on, and respond to the text by answering the following questions.

REFLECT AND TAKE ACTION:

What personal tragedies have you been through? Take time to explain each situation thoroughly.

_____
_____
_____
_____
_____
_____
_____
_____
_____
_____

What relational wounds do you have from your past?

_____
_____
_____
_____

How have your personal tragedies and relational wounds affected you?

_____
_____
_____
_____
_____

> *I remember my affliction and my wandering, the bitterness and the gall. I well remember them, and my soul is downcast within me.*
>
> —Lamentations 3:19-20

Consider the scripture above and answer the following questions:

What stands out to you from this verse?

_____
_____
_____
_____
_____

Can you relate to Jeremiah in this passage?

_____
_____
_____
_____
_____

Have you ever "beaten yourself up" over the past? Do you still do this?

_____
_____
_____
_____
_____
_____

Have you made progress in freeing yourself from the prisons of your past? How much?

_____
_____
_____
_____
_____
_____
_____
_____

Have you ever blamed others for your past pain? Whom and why?

_____
_____
_____
_____
_____
_____
_____
_____
_____

STEP 2

KNOWING MY TRUE IDENTITY

Stop chasing acceptance everywhere else. It's a gift from God. You can't earn it. You must receive it.

READING TIME

As you read Step 2: "Knowing My True Identity" in *Freedom*, reflect on, and respond to the text by answering the following questions.

REFLECT AND TAKE ACTION:

Where does your identity come from?

_____
_____
_____
_____
_____
_____

Have you ever believed a lie about yourself in the past? What was it? Why did you believe it?

_____
_____
_____
_____
_____
_____
_____
_____
_____
_____
_____

Could there be other false labels and lies you are believing?

_____
_____
_____
_____
_____

> *You are a chosen people, a royal priesthood, a holy nation, a people belonging to God, that you may declare the praises of him who called you out of darkness into his wonderful light. Once you were not a people, but now you are the people of God; once you had not received mercy, but now you have received mercy.*
>
> —1 Peter 2:9-10

Consider the scripture above and answer the following questions:

What is the meaning of this passage?

_____
_____
_____
_____
_____
_____

How can you apply the truth of this verse to your life?

_____
_____
_____
_____
_____
_____

Where does true acceptance come from? Is this the only place?

_____
_____
_____
_____

How does one's perspective shift if they know they are accepted?

How should we live knowing that we are accepted and loved?

STEP 3

CHOOSING RELATIONSHIP OVER RELIGION

"How will you become godly?" is one of the most important questions you can ask yourself after you've accepted Christ. The answer determines whether you will have a life-giving relationship or toxic religion.

READING TIME

As you read Step 3: "Choosing Relationship Over Religion" in *Freedom*, reflect on, and respond to the text by answering the following questions.

REFLECT AND TAKE ACTION:

Explain how, up to this point, you have approached getting closer to God. Discuss what the Holy Spirit has begun to stir in you regarding your approach.

_____
_____
_____
_____
_____
_____
_____
_____
_____
_____
_____
_____
_____

Now that you understand the two different trees, discuss which tree you have been living in?

_____
_____
_____
_____
_____
_____

> *But I am afraid that just as Eve was deceived by the serpent's cunning, your minds may somehow be led astray from your sincere and pure devotion to Christ.*
>
> —2 Corinthians 11:3

Consider the scripture above and answer the following questions:

What is the meaning of this scripture?

_____
_____
_____
_____
_____
_____
_____

What is one thing you can do daily to get in or stay in the Tree of Life?

_____
_____
_____
_____
_____
_____

What does it look like when a Christian lives in the right tree?

_____
_____
_____
_____

Sometimes in our pursuit of God we have a tendency to try to work our way into salvation. What one step can you take this week to focus more on Jesus and less on works?

STEP 4

BREAKING THE CYCLE OF GENERATIONAL CURSES

Anything that is not transformed is transferred to the next generation.

READING TIME

As you read Step 4: "Breaking the Cycle of Generational Curses" in *Freedom*, reflect on, and respond to the text by answering the following questions.

REFLECT AND TAKE ACTION:

In your own words, define a generational curse.

_____
_____
_____
_____
_____
_____

Do you feel as if there is a cycle of generational curses you need to break in your life?

_____
_____
_____
_____
_____

Do cycles of generational blessings exist? How do you acquire them?

_____
_____
_____
_____
_____
_____
_____
_____

> This day I call the heavens and the earth as witnesses against you that I have set before you life and death, blessings and curses. Now choose life, so that you and your children may live and that you may love the Lord your God, listen to his voice, and hold fast to him.
>
> —Deuteronomy 30:19

Consider the scripture above and answer the following questions:

What does this verse reveal about generational consequences?

_____
_____
_____
_____
_____
_____
_____
_____

How does this verse change your perspective, if at all?

_____
_____
_____
_____
_____
_____
_____
_____

Will your life be a stepping stone for your family to go higher or a stumbling block that causes them to struggle? Why?

___

How can one avoid generational curses while obtaining generational blessings?

___

How is God calling you to "step out" in your current situation? What's stopping you from obeying His command?

___

STEP 5

HEARING GOD'S VOICE

God does not have a speaking problem. We actually have a hearing problem.

READING TIME

As you read Step 5: "Hearing God's Voice" in Freedom, reflect on, and respond to the text by answering the following questions.

REFLECT AND TAKE ACTION:

Have you ever heard the voice of God? What did it sound like?

_____
_____
_____
_____
_____
_____
_____
_____

How often do you sit and listen for what God has to say?

_____
_____
_____
_____

What in your life could be distracting you from the voice of God? What voices are competing with His?

_____
_____
_____
_____
_____

FREEDOM: STUDY GUIDE | 23

Is your heart prepared to hear from God? Why?

___

> *The gatekeeper opens the gate for him, and the sheep listen to his voice. He calls his own sheep by name and leads them out. When he has brought out all his own, he goes on ahead of them, and his sheep follow him because they know his voice. But they will never follow a stranger; in fact, they will run away from him because they do not recognize a stranger's voice.*
>
> —John 10:3-5

Consider the scripture above and answer the following questions:

What does it mean to "know His voice"?

___

What does it mean that "they do not recognize a stranger's voice"?

___

When you hear God's voice, do you test it against His Word? Why or why not?

When you discern God's voice, do you obey? What is He asking you to do in your current season?

Whom do you have in your life that you consider to be godly counsel? How often do you go to these people?

Take time today to lean in, listen, and move closer to God.

STEP 6

MASTERING YOUR MIND

If your thinking is limited, your life will be limited.

READING TIME

As you read Step 6: "Mastering Your Mind" in *Freedom*, reflect on, and respond to the text by answering the following questions.

REFLECT AND TAKE ACTION:

In what ways have you let your self-image define you?

_____
_____
_____
_____
_____
_____

What major past events have you let affect you? What past events have you overcome?

_____
_____
_____
_____
_____
_____
_____
_____

What has the enemy accused you of being? Did you let him affect you?

_____
_____
_____
_____
_____
_____
_____

> *Those who are dominated by the sinful nature think about sinful things, but those who are controlled by the Holy Spirit think about things that please the Spirit. So letting your sinful nature control your mind leads to death. But letting the Spirit control your mind leads to life and peace.*
>
> —Romans 8:5-6 (NLT)

Consider the scripture above and answer the following questions:

What is the meaning of this verse?

_____
_____
_____
_____
_____

Why is it important to master your mind? What do your thoughts affect?

_____
_____
_____
_____
_____

How do you guard your mind? How can you better guard your mind moving forward?

_____
_____
_____

In your own words, what is "transformed thinking"? Which of the five methods to achieve transformed thinking do you need to implement in your life?

What barriers exist that come between you and the Holy Spirit, if any?

Have you requested to receive the gift of the Holy Spirit and subsequently received Him?

STEP 7

OPPOSING A CULTURE OF IDOLATRY

*Don't try to modify God to fit your culture.
We need to be modified to fit God's will.*

READING TIME

As you read Step 7: "Opposing a Culture of Idolatry" in *Freedom*, reflect on, and respond to the text by answering the following questions.

REFLECT AND TAKE ACTION:

In your own words, how would you define idolatry?

_____
_____
_____
_____
_____
_____

What idols are you struggling with currently or have you struggled with in the past?

_____
_____
_____
_____
_____
_____
_____
_____

Where is your sanctuary? Where do you go when you need help, rest, or peace?

_____
_____
_____
_____
_____
_____
_____

What are some other examples of idolatry in our culture today?

___

> *So here's what I want you to do, God helping you: Take your everyday, ordinary life— your sleeping, eating, going-to-work, and walking-around life—and place it before God as an offering. Embracing what God does for you is the best thing that you can do for him. Don't become so well adjusted to your culture that you fit into it without even thinking. Instead, fix your attention on God. You'll be changed from the inside out. Readily recognize what he wants from you, and quickly respond to it. Unlike the culture around you, always dragging you down to its level of immaturity, God brings the best out of you, develops well-formed maturity in you.*
>
> —Romans 12:1-2 (MSG)

Consider the scripture above and answer the following questions:

What do you think the meaning of this verse is?

___

How can you apply the truth of this passage to your life?

While you may not be required to bow to a statue or be thrown into a furnace, how can you oppose idolatry like Shadrach, Meshach, and Abednego did?

Do you live with a sense of purpose and urgency? What is your purpose? Why do you pursue this purpose with urgency?

Are you "all-in"? What in your life needs to be uprooted for you to be able to say this with confidence?

_____
_____
_____
_____
_____
_____

How often do you spend time with God? Does this reflect Him being your number one priority?

_____
_____
_____
_____
_____
_____

When you encounter trouble, uncertainty, or hardships, do you take them to the Lord? How? Explain your answer.

_____
_____
_____
_____
_____
_____

STEP 8

USING SPIRITUAL WEAPONS FOR A SPIRITUAL WAR

You're either in the battle or in bondage.

READING TIME

As you read Step 8: "Using Spiritual Weapons for a Spiritual War" in *Freedom*, reflect on, and respond to the text by answering the following questions.

REFLECT AND TAKE ACTION:

How can we ready ourselves for the spiritual warfare taking place?

_____
_____
_____
_____
_____
_____

> *For though we live in the world, we do not wage war as the world does. The weapons we fight with are not the weapons of the world. On the contrary, they have divine power to demolish strongholds. We demolish arguments and every pretension that sets itself up against the knowledge of God, and we take captive every thought to make it obedient to Christ.*
>
> —2 Corinthians 10:3-5

Consider the scripture above and answer the following questions:

How does this verse make you feel?

_____
_____
_____
_____
_____

What stands out to you from this verse?

___

Has the enemy constructed any strongholds in your life?

___

What strongholds were revealed in the survey, "Deception Versus Truth"? Where did those lies original begin?

___

Review the seven steps of spiritual warfare to break the strongholds in your life. What did God reveal to you through this process?

_____
_____
_____
_____
_____
_____
_____

What power do we have through Jesus Christ's death on the cross? Do you utilize this?

_____
_____
_____
_____
_____
_____
_____

What can you do today to be better equipped for the spiritual warfare ahead?

_____
_____
_____
_____
_____
_____
_____

www.ingramcontent.com/pod-product-compliance
Lightning Source LLC
Chambersburg PA
CBHW070654100426
42734CB00048B/2990